PAPER PANDA'S
GUIDE TO PAPERCUTTING

Paper Panda & Friends

PAPER PANDA'S
GUIDE TO PAPERCUTTING

Paper Panda & Friends

SEARCH PRESS

First published in 2017

Search Press Limited
Wellwood, North Farm Road,
Tunbridge Wells, Kent TN2 3DR

Reprinted 2017

Print ISBN: 978-1-78221-324-6

The Publishers and author can accept no
responsibility for any consequences arising from
the information, advice or instructions given in
this publication.

Readers are permitted to reproduce any of the
items in this book for their personal use, or for the
purposes of selling for charity, free of charge and
without the prior permission of the Publishers.
Any use of the items for commercial purposes is
not permitted without the prior permission of the
Publishers.

Suppliers
If you have difficulty in obtaining any of the
materials and equipment mentioned in this book,
then please visit the Search Press website for
details of suppliers: www.searchpress.com

Printed in China by 1010 Printing International Ltd

You are invited to view more of Paper Panda's work at:

Website: www.paperpandacuts.co.uk
Facebook: Paper Panda
Twitter: @paperpandacuts
Blog: originalpaperpanda.blogspot.co.uk
Instagram: @paperpanda1
Etsy: PaperPandaPapercuts

Dedication
To my Mum because
she's awesome.
To Roy, my favourite cat.
To Poppy, my darling 13 year old
(going on 38).
Most of all, to my husband,
Ryan, aka Mr P.

Paper Panda

CONTENTS

INTRODUCTION

Hello! If you'd asked me anything about paper or papercutting ten years ago, I would have looked at you quizzically, then proceeded to pour your pint from behind whichever country bar I was working in at the time.

Isn't it funny how life takes you in the most unexpected directions? I was always a crafter in my spare time, but it wasn't until one day in October 2010 that I spotted my first papercut and fell in love. I immediately bought some paper and a set of knives and started to make a basic template to cut out.

It wasn't the huge industry that it is today. There weren't others to ask about techniques and materials to buy, no books and no other papercutters on Facebook (my preferred social network). So I winged it completely, happily chopping away at my paper, leaning on an old box file and watching daytime TV. I was hooked and I haven't looked back since.

My materials haven't changed an awful lot to this day, which goes to show that papercutting is a cheap and easy hobby to begin and that you can't really go very wrong; but this book is here to help you get everything right from the first stage and give you lots of little hints and tips that have taken me years to develop.

Papercutting has recently seen a revival and surge in popularity as many people take it up as a hobby, some going on to develop it into an art-based business, when previously they had rarely even picked up a pencil. You don't have to be a trained artist to papercut – there are thousands of papercutting templates on the market, so there's never been a better time to learn this wonderfully relaxing art form and begin a new hobby. Whether you draw your own designs, make typographical pieces using design software or cut existing templates such as you'll find in this book, there's something here for every skill level and ability.

The first section of the book tells you all about the tools, materials and techniques you'll need, and gives you an insight into my design inspiration. The second part contains beautiful photographs of the finished papercuts (made by yours truly and three talented friends) as framed pictures, cards or just looking gorgeous in a lovely setting! And at the the back of the book are twenty pages of templates that you can cut out, photocopy or scan and use as many times as you wish. Have fun!

Paper Panda x

TOOLS & MATERIALS

ESSENTIALS

Papercutting is a relatively cheap hobby compared to others that require a lot of tools and materials before you even get started. You only need a few basics and other items can be collected over time.

A round-barrelled knife handle

Why a round handle? It resembles a pencil, so it's easier to use than a flat handle. As you get more accomplished with your curves, you'll find that the handle turns in your fingers in micro increments as you go round bends. Round-handled knives are also comfier than the flatter types. Fiskars make a good softgrip art knife for those with delicate hands, but I use a regular Swann Morton Number 1 barrel handle (see right). It's in three sections: the handle, the top, and the thinner blade section, in which the blade is housed.

Surgical grade blades

There are many different kinds of blades available. I use a Swann Morton number 11 which, on initial use, feels bendy and unpredictable, but I find it helps with curves once you are used to it, and it's got a great point for finer details.

Alternatives are Swann Morton ACM 11, 15a and 10a. Try each kind and see which one you prefer. Other brands are available.

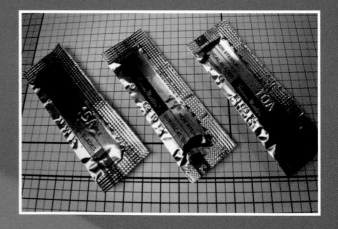

Self-healing cutting mat

You don't need an expensive, fancy cutting mat! In fact, it's best to use a standard, cheap rubber one because they get glued up quickly and wear through after a few weeks of intensive use.

It's good to have two: one for cutting on and one for glueing on. If you use the same mat, then you'll get it mucky and that will transfer to your papercut next time you use it. They can be washed, though. Use a bit of washing-up liquid and a scourer to prolong the life of your mat. When one side wears out, flip it over and use the other side.

Glass cutting mats are popular with some artists. There are some expensive artistic versions, but really a vegetable chopping board will suffice. Don't try this as a beginner, though – it's a slippery surface, and slippery surfaces and knives aren't a great combo!

Paper

Erm, yes, I know – kind of obvious, huh? But the kind of paper you use is really very important! Over the years I've tried everything from recycled elephant poo paper to the hammered 160gsm that I use now. It's down to personal preference, so try anything and everything (except photocopier paper, which is terrible to cut!). We get down to the nitty-gritty about weights and types of paper on pages 14 and 15.

NON-ESSENTIALS (BUT REALLY VERY USEFUL)

A 'pokey tool'

Be it a set of compasses, calipers, sweetcorn skewers, a darning needle or a clay point tool, you'll find life a lot easier with something to make eye holes in your characters, or just to decorate the paper with little dots.

Leather-belt hole punch

This is a fantastic little tool for punching different size holes in your paper for decoration. You can then use the punched-out holes for snow! Get a mechanical punch, not one you have to hit with a hammer.

Blade removal and disposal

You can buy special blade-removal units fairly cheaply, which is the safe and grown-up way of getting rid of your blades. Other ways include getting a 'sharps bin' from your local chemist, sealing them in takeout containers or dropping them into an empty drinks bottle as you go along (seal the lid, recycle, job done).

Tweezers

You can use tweezers to remove old blades from your knife handle (see above), but take great care when doing so. Tweezers can also be used when placing small 'floating' cuts (see page 30) into position onto acetate or glass to avoid getting fingerprints on the easily marked surface.

Metal ruler

This is an essential tool if your hand-cut lines are on the wobbly side. Never use a plastic or wooden ruler, as the knife could slip and cut into them, or your fingers!

Glue

Essential for infills and framing. If you use regular paper glue, you'll find that over time, with exposure to sunlight and central heating, it doesn't hold up. You can use a *tiny* amount of super glue, but this is risky and can show through thinner papers. I use Pritt Power (other stick glues *are* available!) and, so far (*touches wood*), it's been great.

Masking tape

You can use tiny strips of masking tape similar to butterfly stitches to adhere your coloured pieces of paper to your papercut (infills) in addition to glue for extra security. You can also use masking tape to stick your final piece to the frame mount instead of expensive framing tape for finishing.

Anti-static spray

Dust is the framer's nightmare. When acetate is used to float a papercut within a frame, it often attracts dust. It can be cleaned using an anti-static acrylic cleaner and a clean microfibre cloth.

Tracing paper

This is useful for transferring your image in reverse onto your cutting paper.

Acetate

Essential for DIY 'float' framing (see page 30).

Nails

Not the steel type, but fingernails! You need the nail on your index finger to grow enough to hold the paper in place. Yes, really!

CRAFT KNIVES & BLADES

Safety first

I use surgical grade blades that are designed to cut skin. If you touch them, drop them and try to catch them between your thighs (yes, I've done this!), or wave them around randomly, then they **will** cut you very easily. *As always, please keep them away from children and pets, and always store them safely. Respect your blade.*

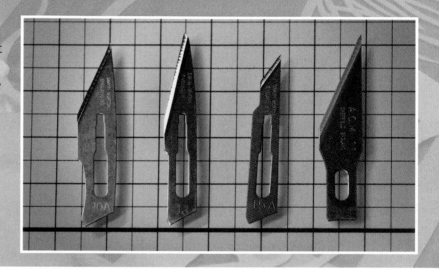

Blade control

Hold the handle as you would a pen, but fairly low down the barrel, as this will give you more control. You can wrap a sticking plaster around the base for comfort, but as you change the blade so often this can be more of a hindrance than a help. Resist the lure of those colourful rubber pencil grips, as they are a real danger to your fingers when you slide them on and off to change the blade. Keep the knife at 45 degrees to the paper and cut pulling it towards you.

As soon as your blade shows any resistance to the paper, change it for a new one. It should cut through like butter. If you scrimp on blades, the edges of your papercuts won't be clean and you risk the paper tearing. I change my blade every 10 to 15 minutes.

PAPER

Paper choice really is based on personal preference. Some papers can be too flimsy, though, so go for paper designed especially for the job, or experiment with speciality papers such as hammered and mulberry (although not mulberry with bits of flowers in – it's a nightmare trying to cut through a piece of rose!)

Really, you can use any type of paper to cut, but I don't recommend anything over 170gsm (see opposite for more info on paper weight), as it's very tricky to cut and will make your hand ache. Photocopier paper and book pages have a consistency that isn't pleasing to cut – you can't get a decent line and it's tough to cut through cleanly; as a consequence, the results can be very poor.

When using paper for infills (see pages 20–21 and 26–29), the world is your oyster: glitter paper, newspaper, lace, a million colours. You'll find that collecting paper will be your new very most favourite thing. It took me a long time to find the right paper for making black papercuts (how do you print or draw the design on the reverse?) – but after a year I found poster paper, which was initially made for classroom walls, but is equally wonderful (if a little thin) to cut. It's white or light grey on the reverse, enabling you to draw or print your design; then you flip it over to perfect black on the front when you've finished. Clever, huh? It does take some getting used to, as when you start it leaves little white flecks on the black side, but keep your blade super-sharp and new, and in time it will improve.

In the meantime, use a black felt-tip pen to fill in any white parts on your final piece (let the pen bleed through from the back, then it's not so obvious). You can, of course, just use a white pencil to draw on black, but that would be too easy!

PAPER WEIGHT

When we talk about the weight of a sheet of paper, what we mean is the thickness, and there are currently two systems in use for paper weights.

In Europe, paper weight is measured in grams per square metre (or gsm), while in North America it is measured in pounds per ream (a ream being 500 sheets). In Europe, photocopier or printer paper is usually 80gsm (not great for papercutting!), and artists' drawing paper is around 150gsm. In North America, printer paper is approximately 100lb per ream, and artists' drawing paper is about 220lb per ream.

If you're new to papercutting, it's a good idea to try out different thicknesses so you can find out what suits you best.

GETTING STARTED

First of all, photocopy this page onto some suitable paper. It contains all the lines and shapes that you will be practising in this section.

Mini squares

Circles

Star

Straight lines

Bunny

Hearts

Practice makes perfect

Before you begin, practise with your knife and see how much pressure is needed to cut cleanly through the paper. You need to apply just enough for a clean cut that goes all the way through the paper; press too hard and you'll get a hand cramp and possibly a broken blade tip. Cut through the lines evenly, taking the time to get the pressure right.

Index finger

I am right-handed. The index finger and nail on my left hand are super-important. They keep the paper taut and in place when I'm cutting. When cutting a very delicate piece the nail comes into play as much as my cutting hand. So, keeping the paper in place with your important index finger, pull the knife along the lines at about 20 past the hour on a clock (or 20 to if you're left-handed, obviously!). This means constantly turning the paper as you cut. Turn the paper at every junction to ensure each line you are cutting is perfectly positioned for you to cut comfortably.

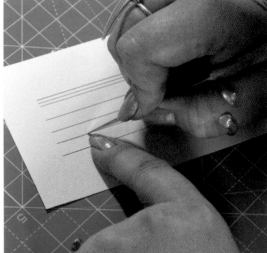

Straight lines

Let's begin with the straight lines. You'll see that the three lines on the extreme right are quite close together (see left). Start with the first line on the left and work to the right (see photographs, right). Holding the paper in place with the index finger of your non-dominant hand, go slowly and carefully, taking care not to rip the paper in between. I find that if you cut a long line all in one go, confidently, then you're more likely to succeed with your straight line.

Don't worry if you wobble off the line; just curl your way back onto it gently, and from the other side you'll hardly notice. Remember, nobody ever sees the guidelines – they are for your eyes only – so they won't know if you've wobbled a bit, because they'll be looking at the finished papercut from the 'good' side.

Circles

You'll either love them or hate them, but curves are an essential part of papercutting, so they can't be avoided.

Your first ever circle will probably resemble a 50 pence piece (a seven-sided coin in the UK), but don't be put off – just keep practising and soon you'll be a circle master.

There's no right or wrong way; some people turn the paper as they go round, while others cut in micro-increments, removing the blade from the paper as they go. I find it easier to cut counter-clockwise.

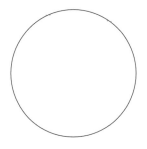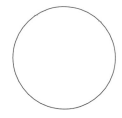

Hearts

It's just another circle with a tea break, essentially. Begin on the apex of the curve down towards the point on each side.

Mini-squares

These are a test to practise not 'overshooting' your lines. Try and keep the spaces between the squares intact so you are left with a nice clean grid.

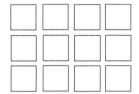

Bunny

When you first start papercutting, stick to natural designs. They are a lot more forgiving if your cutting is a bit wobbly, so it doesn't matter if Bunny is a bit fatter or has a few extra hairs, but it *does* matter if you cut an 'A' off a typographical piece, for example. The same goes for trees and plants – a chopped-off leaf is easily hidden.

Use your 'pokey tool' to make a tiny hole for Bunny's eye. Push it through from the front, not the design side, or he'll have a bulgy eye where the paper pushes through on the good side of the papercut.

Star

Whenever you cut anything with an inner piece of detail such as this star (right), or a letter 'o' or 'e', always cut the centre piece first. It gives you the whole paper to hold on to, to keep it steady, rather than trying to cut the centre out of a floating object.

In this case, you can keep the middle star and use it as a template to create an infill, which leads us nicely to...

Infills and topfills

Infills are covered in depth in the next section (Techniques), but below is a brief step-by-step introduction to a very useful trick!

An infill is where you place a piece of coloured paper behind (or underneath) a papercut for detail, so the colour shows through. A topfill is where you cut a shape and glue it to the top of your papercut to add detail. Basically, these little tricks both add colour and interest to your papercuts. You can use anything from glitter paper to old book and magazine pages. A lot of people avoid infilling because it can be a bit tricky (and messy), but hopefully once you get the hang of it, all of your rainbows will be beautifully colourful.

How to make a simple infill

1 So, you start by taking the papercut star that you made earlier (the middle part that you cut away). We're going to use it as a template. Glue that to the back of some paper in the colour of your choice. I'm using glitter paper.

2 Leave a border of about 3–4mm (about 1/8in) around the star and cut it out. It doesn't have to be neat or perfect – nobody will see the edges. You've now cut a star shape from coloured paper that's slightly bigger than the hole in the original star.

Infilling a tricky papercut

When you've completed your papercut, photocopy or scan it in and print a copy onto regular photocopy paper. Print a copy for every colour you want to use in your final piece. Stick your copy paper to the colour of your choice with masking tape and cut through both pieces of paper together, making sure you cut slightly bigger than the hole you wish to fill, so it covers it and leaves you room to glue in place.

Alternatively, you can print directly onto the coloured paper of your choice, which is easier – but you can't print on glitter paper, so don't pop that in your printer or it'll be messy, like a unicorn Christmas party!

Topfills can be used to decorate your papercut when there isn't much space to cut an infill; for example, just cutting a replica shape from coloured paper and glueing it directly on top of your papercut.

3 Take tiny 1mm ($^{1}/_{16}$in) blobs of glue and stick the infill to the underside of your papercut (the side you can see the lines/template on). You only need small amounts in strategic places – don't get glue-happy, or it will just get messy.

4 Push the infill into position with your knife. If it doesn't stick all the way round, you can always fix it in place later with tiny strips of masking tape, like butterfly stitches for paper.

You can use this technique for any simple infilling; just remember to keep the parts you cut away to use as a template.

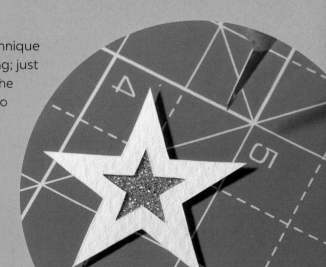

The finished star infill.

TECHNIQUES

MAKING A LAYERED PAPERCUT

Layered papercuts can consist of any number of layers, but just two or three layers can give a wonderful three-dimensional effect that casts beautiful shadows.

Layered papercuts work best when you cut from 160gsm paper, as it holds up on its own nicely without sagging.

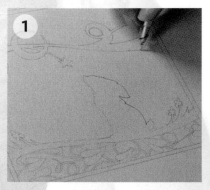

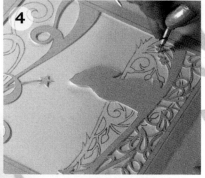

1 Draw around the internal aperture of the mount to ensure the final piece fits nicely into the frame and sketch in your first layer. This layer will be your most detailed and should have a focal point. In this case, it's the hare and the moon.

2 Scan in the drawing and print it onto your first colour. I'm using three neutral tones with the lightest at the front to the darkest at the back to give a sense of depth. If you are using typography, remember to flip your design before you print it. You can just cut directly from your drawing, but it's always good to keep a copy in case you spill your tea on your cut/rip it/the cat runs away with it (not pictured).

3 Once you've cut your first layer, take a second piece of paper (which will be the middle ground) and again draw around the internal aperture of the mount. Line up your foreground papercut with this mount line and, using a small amount of low-tack masking tape, secure it in place (not pictured).

4 Draw in your middle ground using the foreground layer as a guide, drawing in the main details in the available space that won't be obscured by the foreground when in situ.

5 Gently remove the tape and the foreground papercut and complete the parts that the foreground was covering, filling in the gaps in the drawing.

6 Scan and print onto your second colour and cut it out.

7

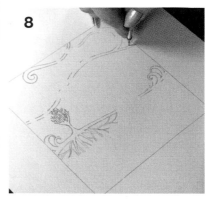

8

9

7 Now you'll have your foreground papercut and your middle ground papercut layers. Tape both of these together to what will be your background layer, again using the mount as a guide to stick them in the right place and draw in your background layer details. This will be the least detailed piece of the three. Pay attention to any gaps you may have left in the overall composition.

8 Remove the tape and the papercuts (foreground and middle ground) carefully. Complete the drawing of the background design. Scan, print and cut.

9 Now you have three layers. Place adhesive foam pads (or sticky dots) around the edges on the front of each cut, starting with the background. Be very careful as once they are placed they are difficult to remove.

10

10 You can also pop the sticky dots in strategic places around your papercut to ensure it doesn't sag in the middle. This can be tricky, so you may wish to trim the foam pads down to very small dots for the more delicate parts of your cuts.

The finished layered papercut with the mount placed over the top.

MAKING INFILLS

Before I began this design I measured the mount it would be framed in and, using a design programme, I drew a rectangle the same size so that I knew it would fit the frame. I added the circles around the edge so then when cut, it would have a perfect scalloped design. I also added a circle at the top (the leafy part of the tree). I then printed it onto hammered paper and drew the design, keeping all of the leaves within the circle.

You will need:
Papercut
Coloured paper
Masking tape
Glue or sticky dots
Backing paper
A knife
Cocktail stick

1 Photocopy your finished papercut or scan it into your computer and print it off. Using masking tape, stick it to the coloured paper you wish to use as your infill.

2 Cut through both pieces of paper in the places you'd like to fill. Make the pieces that you cut out slightly bigger than the hole you want to fill.

3 Once all of the pieces have been cut out, you are ready to glue them to the back of your papercut.

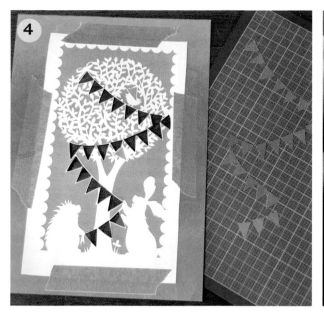

4 Discard any photocopied paper and remove the coloured paper, remembering which piece goes where, and lay it to one side.

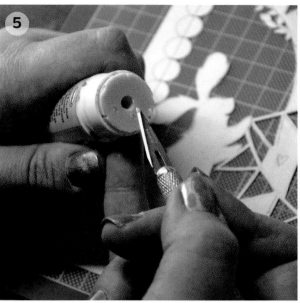

5 Using your knife (or a cocktail stick) take a tiny amount of glue. Too much glue will result in it seeping through your papercut.

6 Place the glue in strategic places as close as possible to the hole you are filling. I always use a different mat for glueing than the mat I use to cut with. This is so that any residue that does end up on the mat isn't transferred to any future papercuts.

7 Position each triangle of coloured paper face down over the relevant hole and stick in place.

8 Pop a strip of masking tape on the side of your cutting mat. Cut very thin strips, like butterfly stitches, and use them as a back-up to the glue.

9 Position the strips gently so that you don't dislodge the coloured paper.

10 Be sure to trim carefully any masking tape that is visible from the front.

11 Remember that you won't see the back of your papercut, so it doesn't matter if it is littered with masking-tape strips like this!

12 The bunting now has all its infills glued into position and is ready for framing.

'Two for Joy'

Lots of different effects can be achieved with infills. The papercut above uses black infills for the magpies; the bee papercut (below left) uses glitter paper, as well as coloured paper, for a bit of sparkle; while the papercut below right uses graduated paper for a more rainbow-like effect.

FRAMING AND FINISHING

You will need:

A box frame
A sheet of acetate
Masking tape
Glue or sticky dots
Backing paper
A knife

You can display your papercuts in a number of different ways. Sometimes it's as simple as using pegs to attach one to a piece of twine or ribbon and hanging it up, providing the paper you've used is sturdy enough. You can use sticky dots (adhesive foam pads) to attach it to a card blank or to raise it slightly in a frame, glue it to a piece of wood and then varnish the whole piece, or you can simply pin it directly to a surface.

Think carefully about your backing paper, as this can change the whole feel of your artwork. You may have used lots of colour and glitter, in which case mounting over an old book page may not work so well. Don't use a backing paper that will overpower your papercut; it should enhance, not detract from your artwork.

There are a lot of different ways to frame a papercut but 'floating' it – where the papercut is suspended in a frame usually between two sheets of glass – is the most popular way, as it shows that it is in fact a papercut and not a print, and it also casts beautiful shadows within the frame. I have my frames made especially for the job using double glass (you can buy them in the Paper Panda shop – *shameless plug*), but you can also create the same effect at home. Here's how...

Floating a papercut in a frame

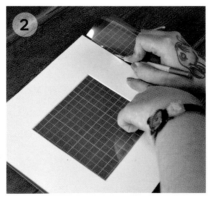

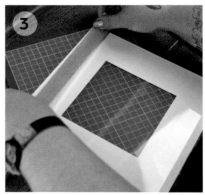

1 Get a box frame, (the one shown is a 'Ribba' by a well-known Swedish furniture shop) and take it apart.

2 Using the mount as a template, cut your acetate to size so it covers the aperture.

3 Tape or glue the acetate to the back of the mount, then turn it back to the front again.

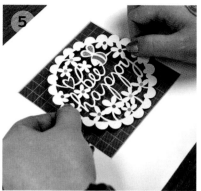

4 Add tiny dabs of glue onto the back of the papercut using your knife or a cocktail stick. Don't apply the glue directly to the papercut as it may rip.

5 Using the grid on your cutting mat as a guide to get the papercut central, carefully place it onto the acetate and press down.

6 Place the mounted papercut into the front of the box frame on top of the glass.

7 Pop in the wooden spacer. You can make your own spacer (if your frame doesn't come with one) using foam board.

8 Using the backing board (or the mount) as a template, cut the backing paper to size.

9 This particular frame only comes with one mount, so you can just glue the backing paper directly to the back board of the frame. An A4 sheet (210 x 297mm/8¼ × 11¾in) doesn't fit exactly, but it doesn't matter because you can't see it once it's all finished. Replace the back of the frame and it's done.

The framed and finished papercut.

DESIGN INSPIRATION

DESIGN INSPIRATION

In every interview I do (not that there are loads, but y'know!) I get asked where my inspiration comes from. The obvious answer is books – old stories such as *Alice In Wonderland* and Grimms' Fairy Tales; but when I actually thought about it, inspiration really does come from everywhere. I have pinned down a few obvious sources that might make you say: "Ooh yeah, I see!"

LITTLE BIRD

The first ever hand-drawn papercut design was this one (see right). I sat one night in my living room with an empty sketchbook and a freshly sharpened pencil and chewed it a bit. I looked around... and spotted my lampshade (see below). Pretty, isn't it? It gave me the kick up the bum to actually draw something and to create the now quite well-known Paper Panda character, Little Bird.

You can even see the position of the red bird at the top of the lampshade, hanging from the branch, that I used in the final design. You'd never think it, looking at both the lampshade and the finished picture, but that's where it started.

The original sketch for Little Bird.

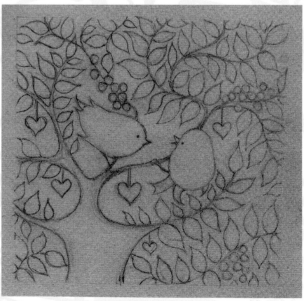

HOUSE ON THE HILL

At the time Mr P and I were listening to Josh Pyke's *Middle of the Hill* song every day – you know how you get hooked on one song and play it to death? Well, that song was ours and, although not particularly relevant to our lives, we did live on a hill – so this papercut was born (see below).

BUNNY

A friend was needed to develop Little Bird's character. There are only so many ways you can display birds in trees, you see, and so Bunny was born.

Why a bunny? I always shrugged and said "Dunno!", but I was being daft, as it dawned on me a year or so later that I woke up every morning looking at this large print (see above) hanging on the chimney breast of my then-bedroom – *Bunny in Boxer Shorts*. So I guess this is where Bunny came from... actually, trying on clothes would make a great papercut! (*gets pencil out*).

Last year I flicked through my old childhood storybooks.
One of my favourites was about a little girl called Matilda
Jane. I based some of my designs (see above) on the layout
of the pages, which had the text in a frame, surrounded by
decoration and coloured drawings.

  I now keep all my old books next to me in the studio
to dip into for inspiration. These have proved to be really
useful resources, and I highly recommend browsing
through books you love to give you inspiration.

JESS AND BROWN BEAR REALLY DO EXIST!

In 2015 there was a Facebook search for Brown Bear who had been lost by this little girl on the right, Jess, on a trip to hospital. It went viral and, yes, she was eventually reunited with her beloved bear.

She takes him everywhere with her. Jess doesn't speak a lot, so I found this little relationship between her and her bear really quite touching, as if they have a secret world together.

The whole thing inspired me to create my Jess and Brown Bear papercut characters, and I have a whole range of papercuts featuring this endearing pair (see below).

The real Jess with Brown Bear.

Use a similar pressure for the knife as you would when drawing with a pencil.
Dan S.

Tea, cake and cracking music are essential! On a more serious note, never be afraid to step out of your comfort zone, always remember that the final piece looks completely different and so much better than that first sketch!
Kirsty H.

Make sure you're cutting in a well-lit area. For the first few cuts I did, I just had my usual living-room light on. When I got a side lamp that I could shine directly over my work area, it helped so much!
Leanne W.

Use old blades and a cheap handle for glueing infills.
Regina N.

Don't forget to take regular breaks – your neck and hand will thank you for it in the long run.
Julie H.

Use good-quality paper and blades to get the best results out of the craft and practice makes perfect.
Jane D.

Everything always looks so much better when cut, and hammered paper is amazingly forgiving. Believe in yourself and have fun!
Emma B.

Cut circles anticlockwise (the best advice by Mrs P so far!), remember to breathe and, surprisingly, poking your tongue out helps!
Laura McK.

Don't be defeatist – you are almost certainly better than you give yourself credit for! And don't dismiss a template for being too hard until you've actually tried it.
Louise D.

If you think your papercut is wonky, skew-whiff or not good enough, stand back and look at it. No one is going to press their nose up to it and papercutting is very forgiving.
Angie L.

Cutting on a tilted surface helped me. It look much strain off my back and neck and allowed me to see my cut properly.
Emily Jane M.

Experiment and try something you wouldn't normally try: new paper, different colours, a different style, fonts or characters. Maybe you'll want to freehand, maybe you'll design your own templates. You'll find your own unique style and you'll enjoy that most. Have fun with it always.
Naz McD.

Never be afraid to try and if it's not right the first time try again. Never throw a piece of your work away that you feel is not good enough; keep it, date it and compare it with your next cuts or use it to look back and see how far you've progressed.
Sammy S.

Beware of RSI. Take regular breaks, walk around and stretch.
Sarah-Jane H.

Be kind to yourself – everyone was a beginner once.
Sara F.

Always recap your knife whenever you leave it, however brief the break. Not doing so is a mistake you only make once!
Fi B.

Don't let the fur babies distract you, they will sit on your work or lap and try to grab your attention.
Tracy G.

Tie your hair back, or get used to scaring yourself (with your scalpel!) on a regular basis when going to tuck your hair behind your ears.
Kayleigh de V.

Make sure you are comfortable and your work area is well lit. Take your time. Start with the most fiddly bits and try to leave the design whole until the end. If you get frustrated, take a break. Don't be overly critical of yourself; stop, look at your work and ask yourself what you'd say to someone else if they had cut the piece.
Donna R.

Shut the door, forget the world and your problems, and relax. Papercutting takes all your cares away for a short while, so immerse yourself in it. Any tension transmits itself onto the paper, so relax and you'll be surprised what a difference it makes.
Susie H.

USEFUL COPYRIGHT INFORMATION

My journey through the minefield that is copyright

This is a subject that crops up a lot in the papercutting community, so I thought that by sharing my experience, it may help people who are starting their own papercutting business to avoid making the same mistakes that I did.

Like many crafty folk, I'd already dabbled in glass painting, card making and other craft hobbies before I decided I'd try papercutting. I made a papercut for myself and uploaded it onto Facebook. Then I made a few more and very soon I had old school friends asking me if they could buy them, so I opened a Facebook page and started trading. Extra money for Christmas – awesome!

This is where I bare my soul – don't judge me too harshly! At the very beginning (first couple of weeks), I used Google images and existing silhouettes to add accents and detail to my papercuts. I thought that the skill was in actually cutting the paper neatly, rather than the design aspect, like: "Look at what I made! See how it's all attached and cut from paper?" rather than: "This design is a reflection of what I was feeling that day and its soft lines... oh, and it's also cut from paper."

After a while I found Shutterstock, a bank of designs and images that you pay for. I had also found some papercutting buddies by then, so we grouped together and bought a subscription. Suddenly, we had all the images in the world! Brilliant. And we'd paid to use them, so it was all good. We assured each other that there were plenty to go round and if A was using that design, then B wouldn't. Excellent. No problem there, then. Or was there? You see, after a while we realised that the images had a bit of small print that said "Not for commercial use". Did this apply to us? Oh dear, yes it did. Scrap that idea, then.

The key was to obtain swirls and accents and to make them unrecognisable from the original, so a bit of a design 'helping hand'. So you take a bit of swirl from one vector, then a leaf from another, and maybe alter the shape a little by tweaking the nodes. That, and we found websites that offered commercial images for designers. Yes, you have to pay a small fee, but if your drawing skills are lacking, then it's the best way forward. I'm not sure the swirls I used were unrecognisable enough

though, and by this time I was a bit spooked and unsure of what I was and wasn't allowed to do. I couldn't draw myself; hadn't done so for 15 years, so I couldn't possibly make drawings good enough for papercut designs.

At this point I decided to make papercuts using just typography. Fonts are pretty in their own right and don't need accents! Hooray! But hang on a sec... why are some free and some not? Here's that 'personal use only' term again. But I use loads of fonts! I have to pay for them **all**? Well, yes – yes, you do. Your papercuts are getting quite expensive to make by this point. I went to buy a pencil.

A customer approached me and asked me to make a papercut based on their wedding invitation. I said yes, of course, but I'd have to alter it to make it my own. So, I redrew the invite, cut it out and it was lovely. I was so proud of myself, I'd drawn my own papercut design! No – no, I hadn't. I'd taken somebody else's original concept and slightly adapted it, which I discovered when the original designer contacted me with a 'cease and desist' formal letter. I had never felt so bad since the day I gave my neighbour a cat-food sandwich instead of beef paste and she ate it (I was 10 years old). I felt sick to my stomach. I honestly

thought I'd done the right thing. I couldn't apologise enough and spent all evening in a turmoil. The lady thankfully believed that my intentions were good, forgave me and helped me with the best bit of advice I ever had, and that I'll pass on to you: **If you are an artist/designer/crafter and you sell your items, then it's your duty to read up and know about copyright.**

I have never been more grateful in my life for a piece of information that seems obvious enough, but it's not. She pointed me in the direction of a book called *Copyright For Dummies* and for a few months I read a bit every day. It was really interesting and, as well as telling me that I'd so far pretty much done everything wrong, it also gave me some excellent tips for my new business.

The lady also went through my gallery and pointed out that the hare from 'To the Moon and Back' was copyright, even though it was silhouetted (the whole phrase 'I love you to the moon and back' has since been copyrighted, too). It turned out that any recognisable song lyrics (that weren't also regular everyday sayings) were copyright. The photographs I'd silhouetted? Also copyright. I dumped 80 per cent of my online gallery into the bin.

After this I purchased all of the fonts that I used regularly. I contacted a few font designers directly and got bulk deals in some cases. I contacted as many of the Shutterstock designers that I could to offer them the profits I'd made from using their designs in part or full as my own, and my apologies for not knowing any better. None of them ever came back to me, probably because they weren't interested in the measly £20 I'd made and I was being upfront and honest.

I scrapped every single old design that 'I' had made and started again – with a pencil and a sketchbook and *nothing else*.

Funnily enough, that's when Paper Panda took off and became popular. It never really was about the skill factor of being able to cut paper (in fact, I know some papercutters who suck at cutting, but they sell really well because their designs are amazing) – but it was about the composition, the drawing, the characters and the originality of design.

I hold my hands up in that I did wrong – I should have read up on the whole shebang before I ever started selling papercuts (or anything else design-related!), but now I know and I wouldn't go back again for the world. Want me to make a Mickey Mouse papercut for £1,000? No thanks – contact Disney.

Now there are thousands of papercutters in the UK and the trend is spreading daily. Many of them go on to sell their wares and good for them; I think it's marvellous. There are lots of papercutting groups you can join that give advice and, hopefully, you'll be told immediately if you're doing something wrong – or you'll read this, and it'll change you for the better. It took me a good long while, trial and error, being shouted at and talking with my papercutting friends before I got it right. Hopefully, you'll get it right from the get-go and will never have to feel the way that I did when I received the email that changed the way I worked forever. (Thank you to the Hummingbird Card Company.)

CREATING A DESIGN

CREATING A DESIGN
DESIGNING YOUR PAPERCUT

You can still papercut even if you can't draw. Yes, really! There are thousands of templates on the market that cater for all abilities that you can buy ready to print and cut yourself. If you'd like to have a go at designing yourself and don't have a pencil to hand (ha!) then try downloading Inkscape, which is a free design program you can create basic templates with.

You can stick to typographical ones or you can watch video tutorials on YouTube and learn how to create all the pretty swirls and decorative objects, too. For lots of lovely font ideas see www.dafont.com, but please respect the usage rights and buy the commercial option if you plan to sell your papercuts.

When designing, ensure that every object is joined in some way to another. The more parts you join together, the sturdier and more successful your papercut will be in the end.

I often hear people saying they can't draw. You'll be surprised, though, at how effective a really basic drawing can be when it's turned into a papercut. Often the simpler, the better! You also get a real sense of achievement when you create your own piece from scratch.

Start with something really basic like a leaf from the garden or a flower (see photograph, below left). Don't look too closely at the detail, just draw the basic form. Use an old botanical journal or an old book page as the backing paper and you'll have a really pretty, simple papercut (below right). You can even photocopy the flora and cut it from that!

Where to begin?

Start with your frame. This may seem back to front but once you have your frame, then you know how large to make your papercut and you can make it to fit. Making the papercut and **then** finding the frame results in 27 (or perhaps more!) papercuts sitting in a drawer waiting to be framed.

Measure the aperture of the mount and use it as your starting point. A 'Ribba' frame mount (see page 30) has an aperture size of 120 x 120mm (4¾ x 4¾in), so make a square that size using a design program, or even use the mount as a template – simply draw round it on your paper. Remember: your sketches may not win any awards, but they will always look ten times better when they've been cut out. Trust me.

SILHOUETTES

Silhouettes are traditionally cut using scissors freehand with the subject standing in front of you. There is a modern-day cheat version, though, that gives excellent results.

Take a photograph of your 'guinea pig' against a plain wall with good contrast, ensuring the whole head is clearly in view.

Resize the photo to fit your frame. You may wish to add a curve along the shoulders using a design package – draw it with a pencil afterwards or just let the design continue into the mount.

Print onto poster paper (black on one side, white on the other) or, if poster paper is too thin for your taste, print the photo onto regular copy paper and secure it firmly to some black paper with masking tape and cut through both pieces together.

Cut along the profile, paying extra attention to any details in the hair or clothes, and add a tiny eyelash if there isn't one visible in your photograph.

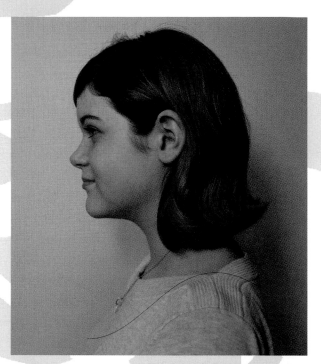

The finished silhouette papercut.

POSITIVE AND NEGATIVE

Are you going to cut into your paper or cut it away? Part of the design process is about the concept of positive and negative elements of your papercuts, as this is a fundamental concept that it is important to understand.

Here is an example (right) of a positive and negative papercut that I drew and cut out from one piece of paper. The positive shape is the piece on the left, which is the silhouette of the girl, while the piece on the right is the negative space - that is, the shape of the girl as a 'hole' in the paper. Both pieces can be used.

I went on to decorate my positive design – the silhouette of the girl – as you can see below.

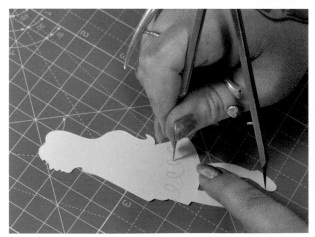

I decorated the dress of my little girl silhouette using my very own trusty 'pokey tool' – a set of calipers.

Here, you can see the light coming through the holes made with the calipers.

TYPOGRAPHICAL PAPERCUTS

If you find the right font, then most of your design work is already done for you. Look for fonts that are joined or handwritten or, if they aren't joined together, then change the kerning (character spacing) in a design program so that

each letter joins to another and is linked so that you don't lose any letters when you cut it out. Remember you'll have to find a creative way of joining any dots above the letters i and j or they'll fall off.

Find a way of linking each word if there's more than one. This can be done by hand after you've printed your letters with some decorative swirls, hearts or stars, for example.

If your drawing skills leave a lot to be desired then have a play with your font. Can you turn an 'S' 90 degrees to make a pretty swirl? The

font shown left is called Pretty Script. The swirl underneath is an 'S' that has been rotated.

When cutting a typographical piece, always cut the insides of any letters first. This keeps the paper sturdy and is easier than cutting the outside first then trying to get to the middle bits. Avoid weeding out your paper detritus until the end for the same reason. It's so easy to rip it when you turn the paper whilst cutting, catching it on the edge of your mat or sleeve. Keeping everything together until the end helps to avoid this.

If you are using a design program for lettering always remember to flip the final design before you print it so that the lines you are following when you cut are on the back and don't show in the final piece. You can also merge or weld the letters together to make it easier for you to see where to cut (see below).

THE DESIGNERS

PAPER PANDA

So, you kinda already know me, but in this part of the book I'm introducing myself (again) along with my friends Sarah, Suzy and Louise, so they don't feel like I've abandoned them. So, I'm Louise Patricia Firchau (yes, Patricia – you heard it here first!) but most just call me 'Panda', which is a shame because I actually prefer cats. I'm coming up to the Big Four-O as I'm writing this. This proves that it's never too late to learn a new skill, and learn it I did (with gusto), and here are the results in this wee book, as well as a few other places.

I did go to art school a very long time ago, but as that involved 6ft (183cm) canvasses and lashings of blue acrylic paint, it was a far cry from anything I do now. So I do consider myself self-taught and, even though people assure me I'm not, I also think I'm a bit of a fluky artist with slightly more luck than most, rather than possessing a natural talent for the arts, but hey-ho... here I am!

My templates are aimed at the beginner papercutter, so are a good place to start before you opt for Suzy Taylor's crazy, complicated-but-completely-gorgeous clock, Louise Dyer's tricky but tip-top tattoo designs or Sarah Trumbauer's constellations (I tried the one with the stars – my word, you have to have some patience, but it's gorgeous in the end!). Mine are quite simple in comparison, and they won't make you throw your knife at the wall and stomp off in a huff... hopefully.

I spend my days cutting woodland animals out of paper in the Cotswolds (a lovely area in the west of England, for those who don't hail from these shores). It's not a bad way to earn a living, to be fair. I hope that you love my little characters as much as I do.

See Paper Panda's designs on pages 58–69 and her templates on pages 112–121.

SARAH TRUMBAUER

I'm Sarah Trumbauer, a papercutter living and working in Pennsylvania. I share my home with my partner Patrick and our cat Lucy. Growing up in a Pennsylvania Dutch family, I learned the tradition of *scherenschnitte* (German for 'scissor cuts') early in life. I have fond memories of my mom and I sitting at the kitchen table cutting parchment paper farm motifs with tiny scissors.

After concentrating on drawing and photography, I decided to experiment with new mediums and I returned to papercutting.

I instantly fell back in love with this medium and found it opened so many creative doors for me. I've been papercutting full-time since 2012 and feel so blessed that I can spend my days making beautiful things to share with you. I find inspiration in nature, fairy tales, children's stories, botanical illustrations and so much more. I am endlessly fascinated by the possibilities of paper and love watching it transform, one tiny cut at a time.

See Sarah's designs on pages 70–81 and her templates on pages 122–131.

SUZY TAYLOR

I'm Suzy Taylor ('Sooz' to my family), known in the papercutting world as Folk Art Papercuts. I knew from a very young age that I wanted to be an artist, although I had no idea what that really meant. There was one particular question that I've always remembered: what do you want to be when you grow up? Without hesitating I wrote: Artist. And as I grew up, that dream didn't go away.

I studied for an academic degree, but the desire for a creative life remained. So I completed a year's foundation course at Chelsea College of Art. A few years passed, and being a stay-at-home mum allowed me to try various creative hobbies.

Around ten years ago I discovered Rob Ryan and papercutting. I had found my creative place. For me, papercutting is the perfect marriage of my love of folk art, obsession with detail and technical skill. Over the years I developed my signature style and my work has become more detailed as I continually challenge myself to produce more complicated pieces. Papercutting for me is meditative and therapeutic. I hope you enjoy cutting my designs and get as absorbed in them as I do.

See Suzy's designs on pages 82–93 and her templates on pages 132–141.

LOUISE DYER

I'm Louise Dyer, artist, creator and papercutter behind 'Paperlace by Louise Dyer'. I live and work in Cornwall from the home I share with my hardworking husband, three small children and a Jack Russell called Denzil.

I've been cutting pretty pictures into paper for three years now. I've always been a creative person, flitting from craft to craft, trying to find my 'thing'. Then, one day in 2013, I happened upon a Facebook page called Paper Panda. I was blown away by her work, purchased her papercutting kit, which received some eye-rolling from my hubby ("What, *another* craft!"), and what I had found turned out to be far more than just another craft. This was something new, something I was good at, something I had a talent for. Papercutting has become my passion and the making of me as an artist. So here I am with a pencil and a scalpel, and some considerable patience. I am influenced by nature and by tattoo art, which is reflected in my designs.

See Louise's designs on pages 94–105 and her templates on pages 142–151.

HOW TO DO IT: PAPER PANDA'S ADVICE

Here are my general instructions for how to go about cutting out your designs. Each one in this book has its own individual tips, but here is what you should bear in mind as a rule:

1 The templates at the back of the book (pages 112–151) all have scissor lines and are printed on 160gsm paper, so you can cut each one out and make your papercut directly from these pages. Alternatively, you can photocopy or scan and print the template onto your chosen paper. Printers tend to copy easily onto weights of paper up to about 150gsm (approx. US 220lbs per ream). You could also trace the image from the book onto paper for cutting.

2 Start cutting the most difficult section of a design first, or the parts that you do not feel confident cutting – this ensures that if you make a mistake you have not wasted much time.

3 Take your time, change your blade every 10–15 minutes and take regular breaks to give your hand and neck a rest. Working on a sloped surface such as a tilted drawing board is a great advantage and much more comfortable than a flat surface.

4 Do not worry about rubbing out pencil marks on the back of the paper, as they will not be seen and erasing may damage the paper. You will be working on the reverse of the finished papercut.

5 Resist the temptation to remove the excess paper as you go along. Keeping it in place helps to stabilise the design and you are also less likely to snag the design on your sleeve/jeweller y/cat.

6 When complete, cut away the excess paper rather than pushing the design out with your finger, as this will stop it from ripping and you can see if any parts need to be re-cut.

THE PROJECTS

PAPER PANDA

1: HOME SWEET HOME

When I was asked to create a series of papercut designs for this book I had a little think and this was the first piece that sprang to mind. Everyone has a home – it may not always be sweet, but in this instance it is, and it'll happily decorate the wall of any home, be it an apartment in California or a cottage in the Cotswolds.

I created the text using CorelDRAW®, flipped it, then printed it and drew in the details with a pencil. It's quite a simple design that is good for a beginner with no scary fiddly parts, so you should get on with it quite well. If you chop off a leaf, heart or a swirl it doesn't matter – just enjoy it, it will still look fab.

See template 1.

2: BRING OUT THE BUNTING

The Woodland Friends are getting ready for their summer party! I wanted to create a design where you could practise your infills without too much difficulty, so here the flags give you the perfect opportunity to add a splash of colour behind your papercut (see pages 26–29 for information on making infills).

I created the shape of the tree by drawing a circle and I ensured that the leaves filled the circle right up to the edges so that it was all in a lovely sphere shape at the end. I cut out a paper triangle and drew around it multiple times to create the flags, so that each one was the same shape.

See template 2.

3: IN THE RAIN

It wouldn't be a Paper Panda book without the characters Bunny, Little Bird and Finn Biddybum Hedgehog! This is an example of creating a piece where I've mixed computer design and drawing with a good old pencil.

I created the umbrella first using curves in CorelDRAW®, added lines for the raindrops to sit on, then added the drops themselves using a pre-existing shape in CorelDRAW®. Copy, paste and repeat a squillion times.

Then I printed it out and drew in the characters by hand. It's good to mix up your methods in this way, especially when you want to create a more uniform look to parts of your design.

See template 3.

4: WITHOUT THE DARK WE'D NEVER SEE THE STARS

I just love this quote – it's one of my most favourite uplifting sayings. I created the text in CorelDRAW®, flipped it and printed it out, then I drew in everything else around it.

I made this with a friend in mind (hi Anna!). So this is Anna and some stars and swirls and it's all very flowing and lovely. But it's terribly curvy so, while there are not many hugely difficult parts, I do suggest you conquer your curves before attempting it. I do hope you enjoy cutting it as much as I did. It really doesn't matter that you lopped off that particular star, it wasn't too important (*cough*).

See template 4.

5: MINI-CUTS:
FOXES, LITTLE BIRD

Here are a couple of small designs that would look great as card toppers for most occasions, or you could frame them as mini-artworks in their own right.

Little Bird is a classic Woodland Friend character, although he's rarely seen without his friend, Bunny.

See template 5.

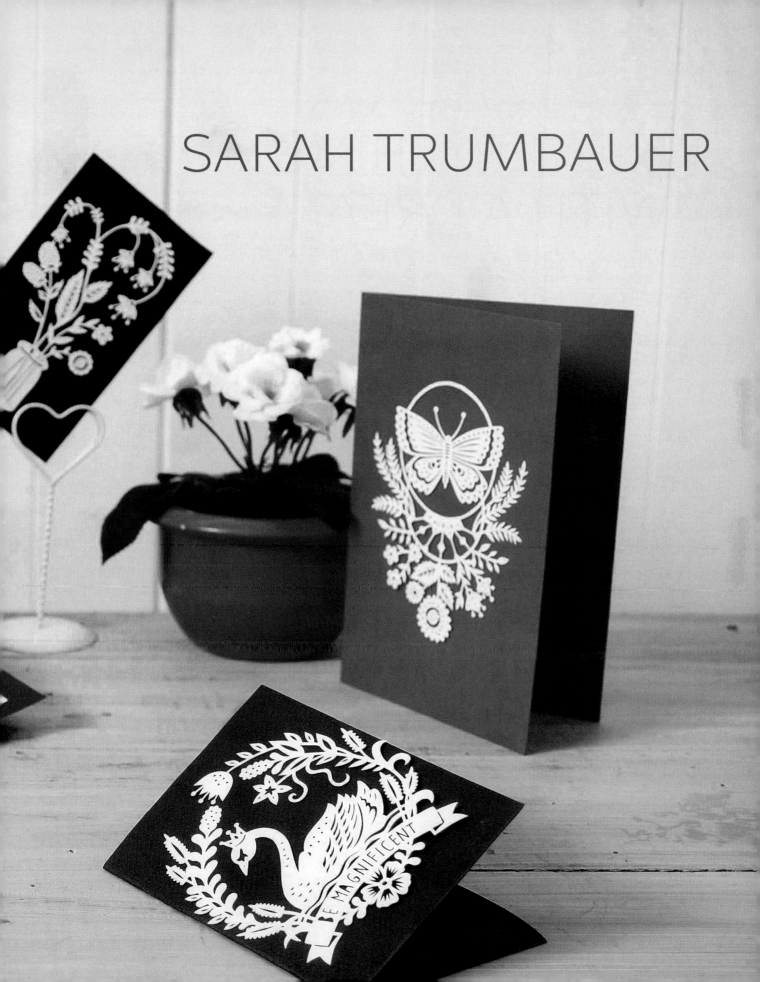

SARAH TRUMBAUER

8: FLAMINGOS

This design was inspired by the amazing flamingos that lived at the hotel we stayed in on a recent vacation to Maui. They were my daily breakfast companions and I knew I had to design a piece in tribute to them.

When cutting, I typically start at the top left and work my way right and then down, similar to writing. This ensures that your hand is not working on top of delicate areas and helps keep the papercut in perfect condition while you cut.

On this piece, I'd suggest working in that manner, but I'd recommend cutting around the flamingos' heads and necks last to minimise the chance of them being bent.

I cut this piece out of my favourite 130gsm white paper, but I think it would also look very striking in black! For backing, I used a beautiful magenta gradient paper, but anything tropical would really bring it to life.

See template 8.

9: MAGIC GARDEN

Before I started papercutting full-time, I was an enthusiastic flower photographer. I was working as a custom picture framer at a camera store and on my days off, I'd borrow equipment and go to the gardens to take hundreds of photos.

  I love flowers and one day I hope to have a garden of my own, but in the meantime we can grow our own little garden in this papercut. I suggest cutting the hanging stars last so they don't get bent, but otherwise I would cut this piece from top to bottom, saving the outer border for the very end.

See template 9.

10: MINI-CUTS:
DECO BUTTERFLY, JAR OF FLOWERS, SWAN

Mini-pieces are so satisfying to cut because you don't have to wait very long to have a gorgeous finished design.

These look great in small frames or on greeting cards and make thoughtful gifts for friends and family.

I've cut all of these pieces out of 130gsm white paper, but they would look equally wonderful out of black paper, especially the butterfly!

See template 10.

SUZY TAYLOR

11: CUCKOO CLOCK

All my designs are drawn by hand on the reverse side of the paper. When designing this Scandinavian-inspired piece, the most important thing for me to remember was drawing the clock face back-to-front – so that it would be the right way round when the paper was flipped over to the right side.

I love the old traditional Swiss-German papercuts and wanted to give this piece the 'feel' of that traditional style, in a contemporary papercut. The birds' legs and the hanging hearts are the most fragile areas – so cut those last and just take it slowly.

If you happen to slice off a heart by mistake, you can repair it with a tiny sliver of tape on the back of the papercut and no one will ever know!

See template 11.

12: FOLK ART CHRISTMAS TREE

I loved designing this piece. I started by simply drawing a tall triangle on a stick in a pot. The branches, holly leaves, berries, flowers and birds all fit within the triangle and I added some decorative designs to the pot as well.

   Cut all the tiny shapes out first – the insides of leaves and flowers, details on the birds, and so on. Then cut the negative spaces between the branches.

   Finally, cut around the outside of the tree. It will be fragile once you've cut it, but when framed will make a gorgeous seasonal piece for your home – or a wonderful handmade Christmas present.

See template 12.

13: HAMSA

The Hamsa symbol is used by many faiths as a protection against evil. It's also known as the Hand of Fatima and the Hand of Miriam.

When designing this piece, I took a lot of inspiration from henna designs. It is quite a delicate and intricate piece – so just take it slowly and don't forget to breathe! Cut all the interior bits before finally cutting the outside of the Hamsa; this will keep the paper nice and stable.

See template 13.

14: FOLK ART PANEL

All my work is inspired by folk art from around the globe. I love the fact that realistic proportions become almost irrelevant in compositions of this kind. Designing this piece was a lot of fun. It combines my favourite things – flowers, birds and a decorative pattern.

I suggest starting your cutting in the central part of the design. Cut all the smallest shapes first and hollow out the leaves and flowers before removing the area around them. Move outwards, cutting the floral border last.

See template 14.

15: MINI-CUTS: DALA HORSE, BEEFEATER, FLOWER PANEL

Designing characters is always really good fun. The Beefeater is a true London icon and I loved the challenge of designing his costume so that he still looked like a Beefeater, even though you can't see the colours of his outfit. The ravens he's holding add a bit of humour and character to the piece.

The small flower panel is designed exactly to the proportions of an ATC (artist trading card). ATCs are miniature original pieces of work, all measuring 64 x 89mm (2½ x 3½in) and will fit into cellophane sleeves.

Like the Cuckoo Clock on page 84, the Dala horse is another Scandinavian-inspired piece – although they are not generally on wheels. I applied some creative licence when adding those, as I thought the flowery wheels added some extra decorative interest. This piece is not too fiddly if you're a beginner and would look really lovely in a floating frame (see page 30).

See template 15.

LOUISE DYER

16: SKY PIRATES

This design was inspired by my mum; we call her the magpie, as she is attracted to anything that shines. This design is a tricky one and I would suggest that you attempt it when you have had some practice at cutting paper. Don't be afraid, though. Approach it with confidence; it is, after all, only paper.

I cut this piece as shown in black poster paper (see Paper Panda's tips for cutting with poster paper on page 14). It's only 100gsm, which makes it a very thin and delicate paper to work with. It is white on one side for printing or drawing your design, and black on the finished side. You can get it in a matt finish (my favourite) or in pearl, which gives a nice shimmer. Black paper can be tricky to begin with, but with practice can yield wonderful results.

I like to tape my design onto my self-healing cutting mat using low-tack masking tape; this prevents any accidental tears or catching. This is my personal preference, but find a way that works for you. If you tape it down to your mat like this, turn your mat to cut rather than the papercut itself.

See template 16.

17: ALWAYS HAVE HOPE

This is Hope. She had been lurking in my sketchbook for some time and when I was asked to be a part of this book, I knew the time had come to finish the design.

Hope is my modern take on a Twenties flapper girl – she is a 'glass half full' kind of girl, like me. Again, I have cut this design in 100gsm black poster paper, using Swann Morton number 11 blades.

Take this one slowly. I would suggest starting with her hair, and moving on to the flower centres, although there is no right or wrong way to go about cutting paper. I like to start with the most delicate parts first, as this works for me.

I think that this design would work wonderfully with coloured infills. All those pretty flowers would be brought to life with some colour.

See template 17.

18: REFUSE TO SINK

This design is heavily influenced by my love of tattoos. Swallows are historically used in tattoos for sailors, each swallow representing 5,000 nautical miles of sailing experience; the most experienced sailors would have two swallows.

Swallows are also home birds; they return to the same location year after year to mate, nest and rest, and for this reason were used to ensure a sailor would return to his home safely.

I have cut this design in black poster paper as with my previous designs, but it would also look fantastic cut in white, perhaps backed in sea blues. The positive message given by this design makes it a great gift.

See template 18.

19: SUN AND MOON

The inspiration for this piece came from a set of Tarot cards I had as a teenager, and the beautiful artwork depicted on them. A sun and moon seemed symbolic of that time for me.

Inspiration for a design can come from all kinds of different places. Once you start designing your own papercuts, nothing will seem the same to you again. A day out with my family has me exclaiming at the pattern in some windows, the design on a napkin, or shouting: "Hold still, kids – I need to take a photo of your silhouettes in this light!"

I wanted this piece to be extremely intricate, like paper lace, and took influence from the now-popular art of zentangles, where pattern meets pattern to create a whole.

I would suggest starting in the centre of this one, taking your time and working outwards to the edges.

See template 19.

20: MINI-CUTS:
ARROWS, BIRD, BEE

These mini-designs make fantastic greetings card toppers, cut here in 150gsm white paper.
   They are relatively simple, so are great as practice projects for the larger ones.

See template 20.

THE TEMPLATES

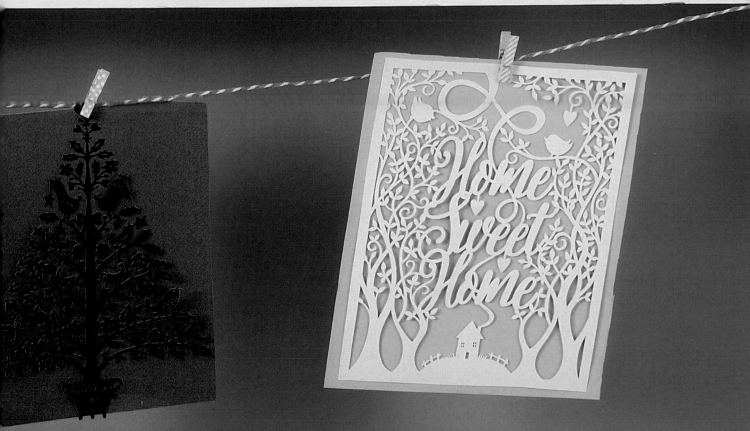

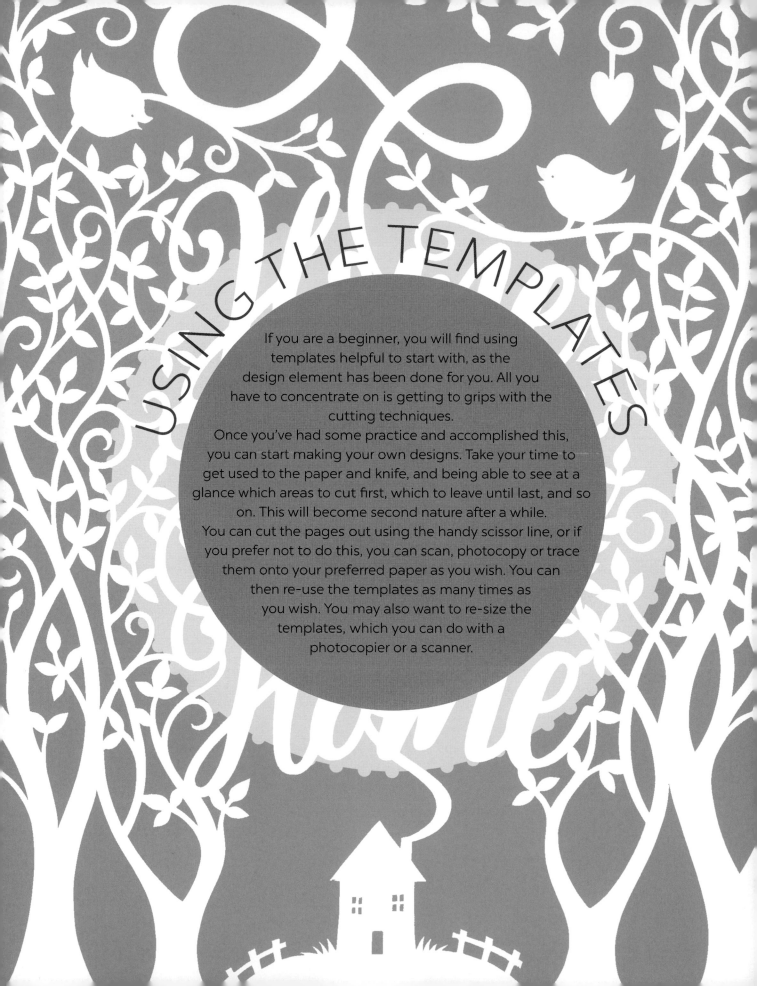

USING THE TEMPLATES

If you are a beginner, you will find using templates helpful to start with, as the design element has been done for you. All you have to concentrate on is getting to grips with the cutting techniques.

Once you've had some practice and accomplished this, you can start making your own designs. Take your time to get used to the paper and knife, and being able to see at a glance which areas to cut first, which to leave until last, and so on. This will become second nature after a while.

You can cut the pages out using the handy scissor line, or if you prefer not to do this, you can scan, photocopy or trace them onto your preferred paper as you wish. You can then re-use the templates as many times as you wish. You may also want to re-size the templates, which you can do with a photocopier or a scanner.

INDEX

The only time you should ever look back is to see how far you've come.

Acknowledgements

There are about half a million people without whom I wouldn't have written this book, but I'm going to pick just a handful because writing the names of everyone who means a lot to me and got me here would take about twelve years.

Big *waves* go to my fabulous admin team, without whom I'd crumble. Seriously, you guys rock.

Rob and Sandra, thank you for thinking we were good enough to illustrate and create artwork for Terry Pratchett and Discworld. It gave us a massive ego boost, huge amounts of confidence and the belief that we can do pretty much anything.

Thank you to my friends Sarah, Louise and Suzy for your invaluable input in creating this book, I couldn't have done it without you.

Huge thanks to May at Search Press for making me think I actually had time to create this book. I didn't, but I'm glad you cajoled me, it's been fun!

You can buy a downloadable copy of the templates on pages 24–25 to make your own Moon Gazing Hare at www.paperpandacuts.co.uk

3

14

17

150